Bible
Puzzles
for
Children

VOLUME 2

Bible Puzzles for Children

VOLUME 2

Ruby A. Maschke

Judson Press ® Valley Forge

BIBLE PUZZLES FOR CHILDREN, VOLUME 2
Copyright © 1991
Judson Press, Valley Forge, PA 19482-0851

Unless otherwise indicated, Bible quotations in this volume are from *Good News Bible*, the Bible in Today's English Version. Copyright © American Bible Society, 1966, 1971, 1976.

Other quotations of the Bible are from *The Holy Bible*, King James Version.

ISBN 0-8170-1165-X

Printed in the U.S.A.

95 96 97 98 99 00 01 02   9 8 7 6 5 4 3 2

Table of Contents

The Bible Is God's Word

People of the Old Testament

Promises God Made

People of the New Testament

Jesus Shows God's Love

Choices We Make

Famous Words from the Bible

We Take Care of God's Creation

We Live as Family

We Worship God

Answers

Fill In the Blanks

Books of the Bible

In order to use the Bible, you need to be familiar with the names of the many books of the Bible. The first five are called the "Pentateuch," or five books of Moses.

Ten **Old Testament** books are listed in Column 1. Place them in the correct blanks in Column 2. The boxed letters spell one book of the Pentateuch, and three others are marked with an asterisk (*). Can you name the missing Pentateuch book? (Clue: It is the first book of the Bible.)

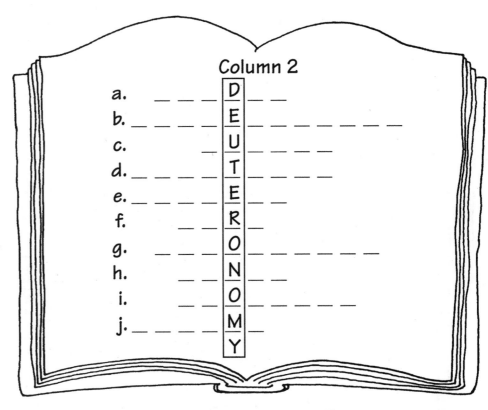

Column 1

1. KINGS
* 2. NUMBERS
3. PSALMS
* 4. EXODUS
5. JUDGES
6. EZRA
7. ECCLESIASTES
8. CHRONICLES
* 9. LEVITICUS
10. PROVERBS

Column 2

a. _ _ _ _ D _ _ _
b. _ _ _ _ _ E _ _ _
c. _ _ _ _ U _ _ _
d. _ _ _ _ T _ _ _
e. _ _ _ _ E _ _ _
f. _ _ _ _ R _ _ _
g. _ _ _ _ _ O _ _ _
h. _ _ N _ _
i. _ _ O _ _
j. _ _ _ _ M _ _
Y

Peter and James are two **New Testament** books, written by the men for whom they are named. The eight scrambled words spell the names of some of the other New Testament books, including the Gospels. Place an X by the four Gospels. The index of your Bible will help you.

1. WREBHES
2. STAC
3. EKLU
4. RAMK
5. HONJ
6. NEEVALITOR
7. WETHAMT
8. UDEJ

P
_ E _ _ _ _ _ _
_ _ T _
_ _ _ E
_ _ R _
J _ _ _
A _ _ _ _
M _ _ _ _ _ _
E _ _ _
S

Putting Things in Order
The Bible Dictionary

A Bible dictionary is usually found near the back of the Bible, or you may have a separate dictionary. It is used like an ordinary dictionary, and explains about people, places, and things.

Arrange the list of words in alphabetical order. If you have a Bible dictionary, look up the words, read the explanation, and write after each word: person, place, or thing.

Jasper	Galilee	Onyx	Marble
Scapegoat	Moses	Goshen	Adam
Covenant	Aaron	Willow	Edom
Moriah	Zechariah	Ararat	Hannah
Topaz	Shiloh	Talmud	Patmos

Look It Up!
The Concordance

There are many books that help us study the Bible. One of those books is a Bible concordance. It has almost every important word of the Bible arranged alphabetically. For example, if you wanted to find the story of God's creation of the world, you would look up the word "Adam" or the word "earth." If you looked at the word "Adam," the reference would be Genesis 2:20; for "earth," it would be Genesis 1:2.

Find a concordance and look up the following:

1. The story of Jonah. You might look up words such as "Jonah," "fish," or "Ninevah."

2. The Lord's Prayer. You could look up "Father," "hallowed," or "kingdom."

3. Suppose you memorized the words of a Bible verse, but now you don't know where to find it in the Bible. Choose a word in the Bible verse, find that word in the concordance, and you will find the Bible book, chapter, and verse. For instance, you know the Bible verse, "God is love." Look up the word "love" in your concordance and find the correct reference.

Find the Bible reference for each of the following verses:

4. "He leads me to quiet pools of fresh water."

5. "They will rise on wings like eagles."

6. "Go then to all peoples everywhere and make them my disciples."

7. "Through faith…they shut the mouths of lions."

8. "Mary…said in Hebrew, 'Rabboni'."

Make a list of some of your favorite Bible stories and Bible verses. Look them up and write the Bible references after each one.

Connect the Words
Adam and Eve

Adam and Eve lived in a beautiful garden called Eden. They were very happy there until they disobeyed God. Read the story in Genesis 3:1-18 (KJV), then write the missing words which can be found in the verse that is given you. Transfer the words to the puzzle maze. The last letter of each word is the first letter of the next word.

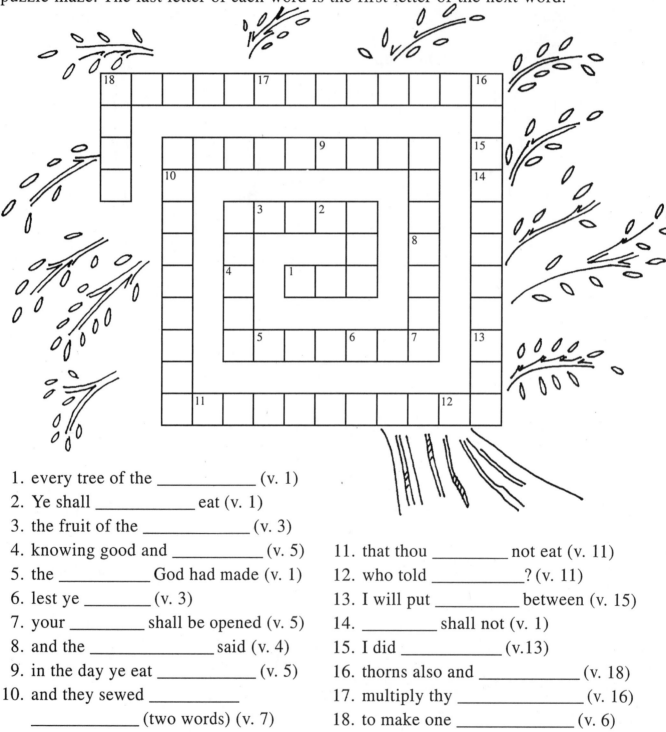

1. every tree of the _____ (v. 1)
2. Ye shall _____ eat (v. 1)
3. the fruit of the _____ (v. 3)
4. knowing good and _____ (v. 5)
5. the _____ God had made (v. 1)
6. lest ye _____ (v. 3)
7. your _____ shall be opened (v. 5)
8. and the _____ said (v. 4)
9. in the day ye eat _____ (v. 5)
10. and they sewed _____
    _____ (two words) (v. 7)

11. that thou _____ not eat (v. 11)
12. who told _____? (v. 11)
13. I will put _____ between (v. 15)
14. _____ shall not (v. 1)
15. I did _____ (v.13)
16. thorns also and _____ (v. 18)
17. multiply thy _____ (v. 16)
18. to make one _____ (v. 6)

Figure It Out!

Noah's Ark

Many years after Adam and Eve lived, the people had become very wicked. So God told a man named Noah to build a boat called an ark.

Work the arithmetic puzzles to learn some facts about the story. Write your answers in the boxes.

1. Noah was _____ years old when the flood began.

    3 + 3 = _____ x 100 = ☐

2. The ark was _____ feet long.   4 x 100 = _____ + 50 = ☐

3. The ark was _____ feet wide.   7 x 10 = _____ + 5 = ☐

4. The ark was _____ feet high.   3 x 3 = _____ x 5 = ☐

5. Besides Noah's wife, he took his _____ sons
   and their wives into the ark.   3 x 5 = _____ − 12 = ☐

6. Noah took _____ of each kind of bird and animal into the ark.

    2 x 10 = _____ − 18 = ☐

7. It rained for _____ days and nights.   8 x 10 = ___ ÷ 2 = ☐

8. After about _____ months, the ark settled on Mount Ararat.

    4 x 6 = _____ − 10 = _____ ÷ 2 = ☐

9. After about _____ months, other mountaintops could be seen.

    50 + 50 = _____ Drop one zero. ☐

10. After about _____ months, Noah and his family were able to leave the ark.

    4 x 5 = _____ − 6 = ☐

Then Noah built an altar on the dry land and brought an offering to God. God made a covenant (promise) to Noah that God would never again flood the whole earth. As a sign of the covenant, God promised to put something in the sky. Work the puzzle below, adding and subtracting letters, to find out what God put in the sky.

— T + — F + — L =

___ ___ ___ ___ ___ ___ ___

Fit the Words

Joseph's Family

There was a famine in <u>Canaan</u> where Joseph's <u>family</u> lived. Many years before the famine, Joseph's brothers had sold him to some <u>merchants</u>. They thought they would never see <u>Joseph</u> again. When the famine came, Joseph's ten <u>brothers</u> went to Egypt for food, and Joseph recognized them, although they did not know him.

Joseph sent <u>one</u> of them back to Canaan with orders to <u>bring</u> <u>his</u> father, <u>Jacob</u>, and youngest brother, Benjamin, back to <u>Egypt</u>. When they were all <u>together</u> again, Joseph told them who he was and that he forgave them.

Joseph knew God had <u>brought</u> him to Egypt to save many people during the <u>famine</u>. Later, Joseph and his brothers became known as the "Twelve <u>Tribes</u> of Israel."

Place the underlined words in the puzzle blanks below.

12

Climb the Mountain
Moses

Many years after Joseph died, the Israelites became slaves. Moses led them out of Egypt, and while they were in the wilderness, God gave Moses the Ten Commandments on Mount Sinai.

See if you can climb up the mountain by rearranging the letters of each word and changing just one letter at a time. The definitions will help, but be sure to start at the bottom! The first letter of each word is given.

Definitions

1. A heap
2. What you can hear
3. Ups and _____
4. Breezes
5. Orange peels
6. Showers in the sky
7. Mountain Moses climbed

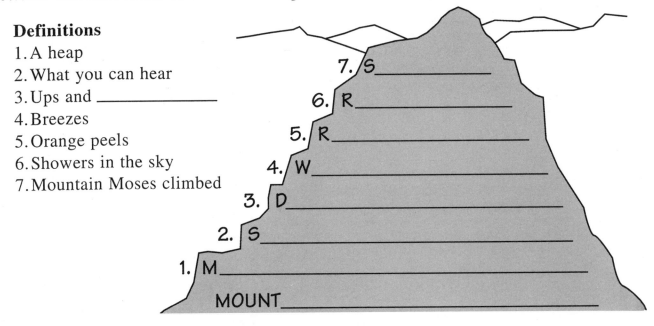

7. S_____
6. R_____
5. R_____
4. W_____
3. D_____
2. S_____
1. M_____
MOUNT_____

Once while in the wilderness, the Israelites needed water. Climb the next mountain to find what God told Moses to use to make water flow from a rock.

Definitions

1. When you cry, you shed_____
2. Kind of meat, beef_____
3. Little Boy Blue slept under a hay_____
4. What Moses hit the rock with_____

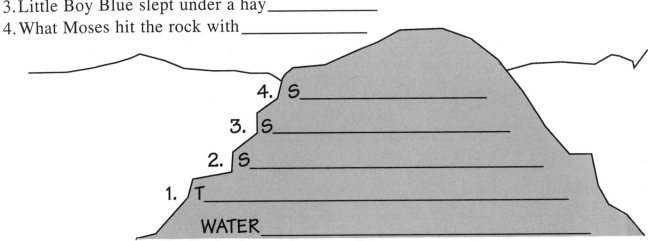

4. S_____
3. S_____
2. S_____
1. T_____
WATER_____

13

A Prayer in Code
Hannah's Prayer

A woman named Hannah had no children. She prayed for a son and promised God she would give the child to the Lord. God answered Hannah's prayer and the baby was named Samuel. When Samuel was still a little boy, Hannah took him to the temple and he lived there and helped serve the Lord. Hannah said a prayer of thanksgiving.

Use the code to read part of Hannah's prayer.

A	B	C	D	E	F	G	H	I	J	K	L	M	N	O	P	R	S	T	U	W	Y
°	!	@	#	$	%	¢	&	*	+	[	"	¶	?	/	]	<	>	§	©	=	£

Hannah prayed, “ § & $ " / < #   & ° >   % * " " $ #   ¶ £
_ _ _   _ _ _ _   _ _ _   _ _ _ _ _   _ _

& $ ° < §   = * § &   + / £   & / =   & °]] £   *   ° ¶
_ _ _ _ _   _ _ _ _   _ _ _ ;   _ _ _   _   _ _

! $ @ ° © > $ / %   = & ° §   & $ & ° >   # / ? $
_ _ _ _ _ _ _   _ _   _ _ _ _   _ _   _ _ _   _ _ _ _ !

*   " ° © ¢ &   ° §   ¶ £ $? $ ¶ * $ >   & / =
_   _ _ _ _ _   _ _   _ _   _ _ _ _ _ _ ;   _ _ _

+ / £ % © "   *   ° ¶   ! $ @ ° © > $ ¢ / #   & ° >
_ _ _ _ _ _   _   _ _   _ _ _ _ _ _ _   _ _ _   _ _ _

& $ "] $ #   ¶ $? /   / ? $ * >   & / " £
_ _ _ _ _ _   _ _ !   _ _   _ _ _   _ _   _ _ _ _

" * [$ § & $ " / < #   § & $ < $ * >   ? / ? $
_ _ _ _   _ _ _   _ _ _ _ ;   _ _ _ _ _   _ _   _ _ _ _

" * [$ & * ¶
_ _ _ _   _ _ _ .”

Find the Way
David's Nation

When David was in his teens, God sent the prophet Samuel to bless David. After that David did many good things. He became a king and made Israel a strong nation. Find the path through the maze and read what each picture means.

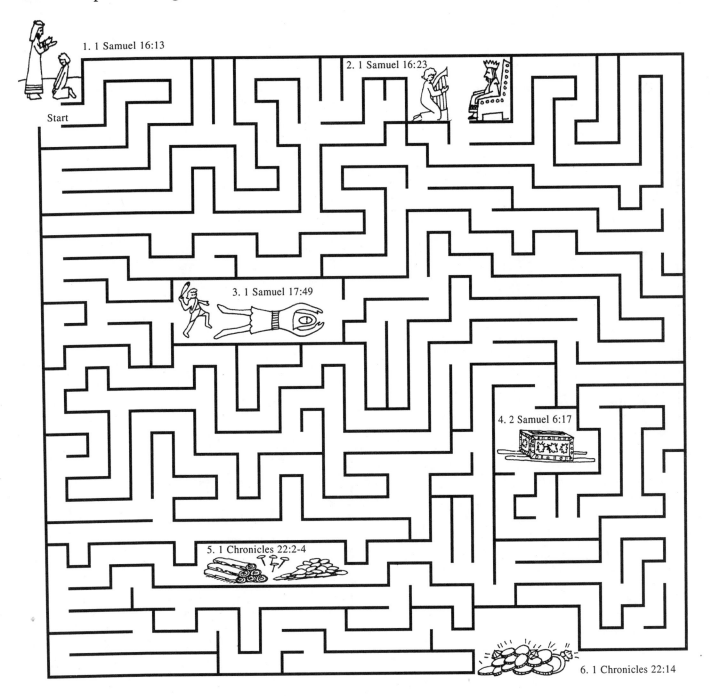

1. 1 Samuel 16:13

Start

2. 1 Samuel 16:23

2. 1

3. 1 Samuel 17:49

4. 2 Samuel 6:17

5. 1 Chronicles 22:2-4

6. 1 Chronicles 22:14

Make a Map
Israel's Twelve Tribes

    Israel was a great nation, but after King David's son Solomon died, the people divided into two countries, Israel and Judah.

    Below is a list of the names of the Twelve Tribes of Israel. Use the list to unscramble the names after the numbers. Then place the names on the map according to the numbers. The heavy line separates Israel and Judah.

Gad	1. NOMEIS	_____
Asher	2. HUDAJ	_____
Issachar	3. AND	_____
Manasseh	4. JIMENBAN	_____
Dan	5. PREMIAH	_____
Simeon	6. SHEMSAAN	_____
Ephraim	7. SHIRCAAS	_____
Zebulun	8. BUZENUL	_____
Judah	9. RASHE	_____
Reuben	10. HALTIPAN	_____
Naphtali	11. ADG	_____
Benjamin	12. NUBERE	_____

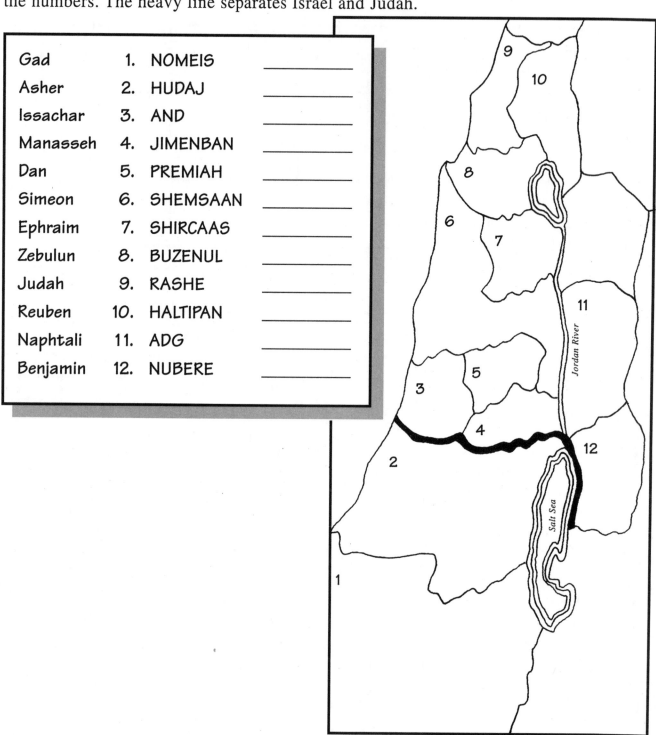

16

Use the Clues
The Fire's Survivors

In the country of Babylon, King Nebuchadnezzar made a new law. Anyone who would not worship a golden image would be thrown into a furnace. Three Israelite men worshiped the true God anyway.

To find the names of the three brave men, follow the clues that are given below. Then write the name on the line beneath each set of clues.

1. Sound meaning "Be quiet!" _____
2. Abbreviation for advertisement. _____
3. 18th letter of the alphabet. _____
4. A pain, minus the "e". _____
   a. _____

1. Myself. _____
2. She minus "e". _____
3. First letter of the alphabet. _____
4. Place to sit, minus "air". _____
   b. _____

1. First letter of alphabet. _____
2. A place to sleep. _____
3. Holds up your head, minus "ck". _____
4. Ready, set, _____!
   c. _____

The three men were thrown into the furnace and were not harmed. Why? Find the answer in the picture. You can read the entire story in Daniel 3.

Write the Words
Daniel's Explanation

Daniel was a very brave man. He was taken to Babylon to be a slave, but God helped him become very important to the kings of Babylon. When Daniel was an old man, King Belshazzar saw a hand write some words on a wall. Daniel told the king what the words meant.

In Column 2 write the definitions of the words in Column 1. The boxed letters will spell the words that were written on the wall. Write these words in the blanks at the bottom and read what each word meant.

Column 1

1. More than one man
2. A fuzzy fruit
3. _____ Belshazzar
4. A red vegetable

5. A disciple, Simon _____
6. Opposite of right
7. It says, "Quack, quack."
8. A bright color
9. Peanut butter and _____

10. Opposite of down
11. An _____ core
12. A large boat
13. An animal that purrs
14. The _____'__ Prayer
15. Opposite of first
16. _____ can
17. It's sweet to eat.

Column 2

a.

b.

c.

a. _____ God has numbered the days of your kingdom and finished it.

b. _____ You are weighed in the balances and found wanting.

c. _____ Your kingdom is divided and is given to the Medes and Persians.

18

A Ladder to Climb

Jacob's Dream Is God's Promise

A man named Jacob traveled from the land of Canaan to a place called Haran. At night he gathered some stones for a pillow and fell asleep. As he slept, he dreamed about a ladder that reached from earth to heaven, with angels of God ascending and descending. When Jacob awoke, he said, "The Lord is here. He is in this place and I didn't know it." Then he made a pillar of stones and named the place Bethel.

The following clues will help you to fill in the blanks on the ladder.

1. Land that Jacob left.
2. Time of his dream.
3. What Jacob was doing between Canaan and Haran.
4. Name Jacob gave to place of his dream.
5. One who visited Jacob.
6. Angels were ascending and_____.
7. Jacob _____ on the ground.
8. _____s were on the ladder.
9. He _____the resting spot.
10. "The Lord is here! He is in this _____!"
11. Place Jacob was going to.

19

A Promise in the Stars

God's Promise to Abraham

In the book of Genesis we can read about Abraham. God said to Abraham, "I will give you many descendants, and they will become a great nation" (Genesis 12:2). On the lines below, write the words in the stars in order by number. Then read a wonderful promise God made to Abraham.

_____

_____

_____

Fill In the Words
God Continues the Promise Through Moses

God chooses people to carry out God's promises. God promised Abraham that he would be the ancestor of many people. Through Moses, God promised the people a special land.

To find out more about that land, fill in as many words in the Word Column as you can. Then transfer the letters to the blanks below, matching the numbers.

WORD COLUMN

a. cooked in oven

— — — — —
17 10 50 15 35

b. stumbled (two words)

— — — —   — — — —
19 57 32 4   9 38 43 11

c. boat being pushed by wind is _____

— — — — — — —
6 51 40 16 48 34 14

d. light at night

— — — — — — — — —
47 55 30 8 5 44 42 24 29

e. opposite of overhead

— — — — — — — — — —
27 13 53 7 21 56 26 31 45 54

f. baby deer

— — — —
36 33 2 28

g. small mountain

— — — —
46 3 37 49

h. small city

— — — —
23 20 39 52

i. large bird

— — — — —
22 12 14 4 25

j. very small

— — — —
29 1 41 58

k. myself

— —
47 18

God said, " __   — — — —   — — — —   — —   — — — — —
     1   2 3 4 5   6 7 8 9   10 11   12 13 14 15 16

— — — — — —   — — — — . . — — — —   — —   — — — —
17 18 19 20 21 22   23 24 25 26   27 28 29 30   31   32 33 34 35

— — — — — — —   — — — —   — — — —   — — —   — — — — — ."
36 37 38 39 40 41 42   43 44 45 46   47 48 49 50   51 52 53   54 55 56 57 58

21

It's a Maze!

Entering the Promised Land

After Moses died, a man named Joshua was the leader of the Israelites. He sent some spies to the town of Jericho and a woman helped them escape. Next God parted the waters of the Jordan River so the people could cross it. Then the Israelites blew on trumpets and the walls of Jericho fell down. Find the path that leads to each event. If you would like to read more about what happened, look up the Bible references given.

Start

Joshua 2:15

Joshua 3:16

Joshua 6:20

Unscramble the Scrambles
Mary's "Magnificat"

Before Jesus was born, an angel came to a young woman named Mary, and said, "Behold, thou shalt conceive in thy womb, and bring forth a son, and shalt call his name Jesus. He shall be great, and shall be called the Son of the Highest:…and of his kingdom there shall be no end" (Luke 1:30-33, KJV). Then Mary told her cousin, Elizabeth, how happy she was. Her song is called the "Magnificat."

Unscramble the underlined words below to see what Mary said. You may want to look up the verses in Luke 1:46-55 (KJV).

Verse 46 And Mary said, My soul doth Y A I M F N G _ _ _ _ _ _ _ the Lord,

Verse 47 And my T I S R P I _ _ _ _ _ _ hath rejoiced in God

my R A I S V U O _ _ _ _ _ _ _.

Verse 48 For he hath regarded the low T S A E E T _ _ _ _ _ _ of his handmaiden:

for, E H B L O D _ _ _ _ _ _, from henceforth all generations

shall call me D E S B E L S _ _ _ _ _ _ _.

Verse 49 For he that is TI M H Y G _ _ _ _ _ _ hath done to me

T R A E G _ _ _ _ _ things; and holy is his name.

Verse 50 And his C M R Y E _ _ _ _ _ is on them that E R F A _ _ _ _

him from generation to generation.

Verse 51 He hath shewed R N T E H S T G _ _ _ _ _ _ _ _ with his arm;

he hath scattered the R U P O D _ _ _ _ _ in the imagination of

their S E R H A T _ _ _ _ _ _.

Verse 52 He hath put O N W D _ _ _ _ the mighty from their

T E S S A _ _ _ _ _, and exalted them of low degree.

Verse 53 He hath filled the G N H R U Y _ _ _ _ _ _ with good things; and the rich

he hath sent Y T E P M _ _ _ _ _ away.

Verse 54 He hath holpen his servant S A I E R L _ _ _ _ _ _ , in remembrance

of his C M R E Y _ _ _ _ _;

Verse 55 As he spake to our S E T F H A R _ _ _ _ _ _ _, to Abraham,

and to his D E S E _ _ _ _ for ever.

Letters to Add and Subtract
The Wise Men's Journey

Add and subtract letters as directed to find each word. Place the new words in the blanks in the paragraph to read about some men who were looking for Jesus.

1. SCHOOL - L + UNDER - SHORE + STRAY - SAD = _____

2. BETTY + H + LEAN - ANY + HEM - T = _____

3. SAT + UNDER - NEAR + I + BREAD - BAR = _____

4. IS + TALL - ILL + HORSE - HOE = _____

5. SKEIN + GATE - TEASE = _____

6. SHELL + TRAIN - STALL + POD - PIN = _____

7. END + CLAIM - DIN + SOUND - MOUND + TIP - CLIP = _____

8. SWIM + TORE - TIMES + ASH + TIP - AT = _____

9. LEG + MOON - LEMON + LAMP - MAP + D = _____

10. FRAME + N + KING - G

    + CENTS - STEM + HOSE - OH = _____

11. MONKEY - ONE + CARROTS - SACK + SHOE - TOES - O = _____

In a (1) _____ far from (2) _____

lived some wise men who (3) _____ the (4) _____ .

They went to Jerusalem and asked (5) _____ (6) _____ ,

"Where is the King of the Jews? We have seen his star in the (7) _____

and have come to (8) _____ him." The wise men brought gifts of

(9) _____ , (10) _____

and (11) _____ .

Circle Words
The Disciples of Jesus

Jesus had a special reason for choosing twelve men to be his disciples. You can read that special reason by writing the "circle words" in the spaces beside the circles.

You did not (CHOOSE) _____ me; I chose you, and

(APPOINTED) _____ you to go and (BEAR) _____

much fruit, the kind of (FRUIT) _____ that endures. And so the

(FATHER) _____ will (GIVE) _____

you whatever you (ASK) ___ of him in my (NAME) _____ .

Now write the names of the disciples where they fit in the blanks. The boxed letters will spell the name of another disciple. The name of the twelfth disciple is missing. Do you know who it was?

1. THOMAS   _ _ _|B|_ _ _
2. JOHN   _ _ _ _
3. PETER   _ _ _ _ _
4. MATTHEW   _ _ _ _ _ _ — S
5. JAMES   _ _ _ _ _
6. JAMES   _ _ _ _ _
7. SIMON   _ _ _ _ _
8. ANDREW   J _ _ _ _ _
9. PHILIP   _ _ _ _ _ _
10. THADDAEUS   _ _ _ _ _ _

25

1, 2, 3...
How Joanna Helped

The Bible does not tell us much about Joanna, but we know some of the things she did that tell us what kind of person she was.

Write all of the words in the squares marked 1; then continue with the squares marked 2, and then with 3, 4, and 5, to find out more about Joanna.

1 When	2 women	3 Joanna	4 Jesus	5 was	1 Jesus	2 supported	3 and
4 had	5 empty,	1 was	2 his	3 some	4 been	5 and	1 teaching
2 work	3 other	4 placed	5 an	1 and	2 and	3 women	4 after
5 angel	1 preaching,					2 helped	3 went
4 he	5 told					1 Joanna	2 him.
3 to	4 was					5 them	1 and
2 On	3 the	4 crucified.	5 Jesus	1 many	2 Easter	3 tomb	4 The
5 was	1 other	2 morning,	3 where	4 tomb	5 alive.		

_____

_____

_____

_____

_____

You can show your faith in and love for Jesus by the things you do.

Picture Clues
Philip

A man named Philip told people about Jesus and was used by God to heal many people. Once an officer of the Queen of Ethiopia needed someone to help him with something he was reading.

Use the pictured clues to read how Philip helped the Ethiopian. You can read the story in the Bible, in Acts 8:26-39.

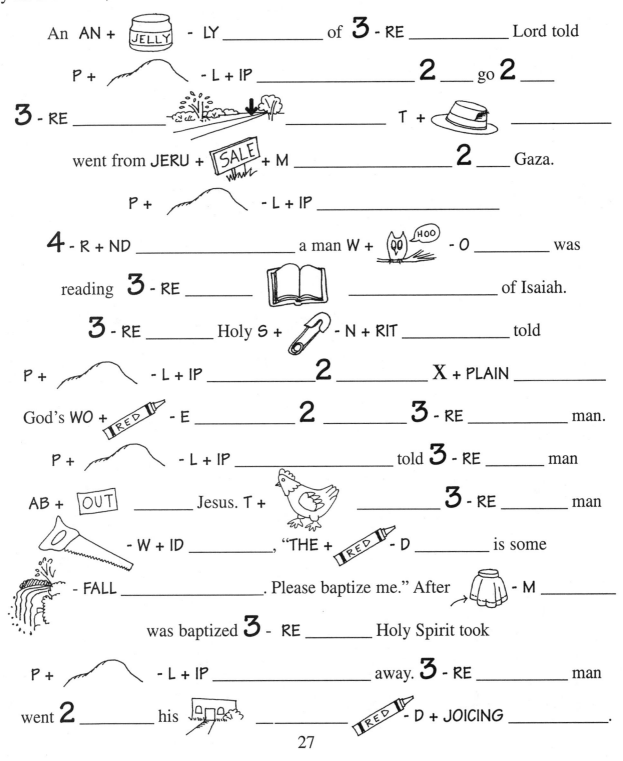

An AN + [JELLY] - LY _____ of **3** - RE _____ Lord told

P + ⛰ - L + IP _____ **2** ___ go **2** ___

3 - RE _____ 🌿⬇🌳 _____ T + 🎩 _____

went from JERU + [SALE] + M _____ **2** ___ Gaza.

P + ⛰ - L + IP _____

4 - R + ND _____ a man W + 🦉(HOO) - O _____ was

reading **3** - RE ___ 📖 _____ of Isaiah.

3 - RE ___ Holy S + 📌 - N + RIT _____ told

P + ⛰ - L + IP _____ **2** _____ X + PLAIN _____

God's WO + [RED] - E _____ **2** _____ **3** - RE _____ man.

P + ⛰ - L + IP _____ told **3** - RE ___ man

AB + [OUT] _____ Jesus. T + 🐔 _____ **3** - RE ___ man

🪚 - W + ID _____, "THE + [RED] - D _____ is some

〰 - FALL _____. Please baptize me." After 👗 - M _____

was baptized **3** - RE _____ Holy Spirit took

P + ⛰ - L + IP _____ away. **3** - RE _____ man

went **2** _____ his 🏠 _____ [RED] - D + JOICING _____.

Combine the Letters
Peter

After Jesus ascended into heaven, his followers preached to many people. Sometimes those followers were arrested and imprisoned.

Combine the small letters with each large letter to form a word, and read what happened to one disciple.

Rhyme Puzzles
Lydia

Work each of the rhyme puzzles below, using the new words you find to fill the blanks in the paragraph.

1

I'm a letter and also a drink	____
Not in KNIT but find me in THINK	____
I'm before Z in the alphabet	____
You'll find me in SEAT, not in SET	____
In the alphabet I come after S	____
I sound like EYE. Can you guess?	____
Say M N O P Q and	____
You see me in LAP and also in CAR	____

2

You see me in PLAIN not in NAIL	____
I'm in TRAIL, but never in TAIL	____
I'm not in RAT, but see me in RATE	____
First in the alphabet, I appear in ATE	____
I'm once in CAT and twice in CATCH	____
I'm once in CHAT and twice in HATCH	____

3

See me in TABLE but not in LATE	____
I'm not in PELT, just in PLATE	____
I appear in SPIN, but not in SIN	____
You find me in PINT, not in PIN	____
I'm not in RAP, but see me in PAIR	____
I'm in RAZED but not in DARE	____
I'm twice in WEED, once in DEW	____
See me in WEND but not in NEW	____

4

See me in BOOTH but not in BOOT	____
I'm once in HOT and twice in HOOT	____
Find me in DUEL but never in LED	____
Twice in SLEDS, just once in SLED	____
Twice in SPEED and once in SPED	____

A woman named Lydia lived in the city of (1)_____.

She heard Paul (2)_____and learned

that Jesus was her Savior. She was (3)_____ and

so were all the people of her (4)_____.

A House of Words
Jesus Healed a Man Who Could Not Walk

A man was sick with an illness called palsy and he could not walk. Jesus was preaching in a home, and it was so crowded the sick man could not get to Jesus.

To read the rest of this story, unscramble the underlined words. Then place those words in the "house." A vowel in each word is in place.

Four of the man's friends opened up the roof and let the man down to Jesus.

Jesus said, "My N O S _____ your N I S S _____ are forgiven."

But some men asked, "H W O _____ can R O I E F G V _____ sins

but God N Y O L _____?" Jesus asked whether it was easier

to forgive sins or to tell the man to walk. Then he told the man

to C I P K _____ up his mat and go E O M H _____,

and the man was D A H L E E _____.

Big and Little Letters
Ten Men

God loves all persons, even when they are not thankful for blessings. The following story will tell you about a time when some men forgot to thank Jesus for healing them. You will need to unscramble the letters within (and including) the big letters to make the words.

In a place called  Jesus met ten men who had _____ .

And they lifted up their _____ and said, "Jesus, _____ ,

have mercy on us." Jesus told them to show themselves

to the _____ and as they went, they were _____ .

But only one of them turned back to say,

Find the Tens

Jesus and the Children

Sometimes Jesus grew tired as he went from town to town teaching and healing people. One day some young children were brought to Jesus. The disciples thought Jesus was too tired to talk with the children.

To find out what Jesus said, find all the squares in which the numbers total 10. Place the letters from those squares in the blanks below.

5 + 5 L E T	2 + 7 B G M	2 + 8 T H E	3 + 4 C H N	2 x 3 D J P	11 - 1 C H I	8 + 1 F L Q
4 + 6 L D R	2 + 6 G L R	3 + 4 H M S	12 - 2 E N C	1 + 6 J N T	7 - 1 K P V	7 + 3 O M E
9 + 1 T O M	2 x 5 E A N	2 + 4 L Q W	8 + 2 D D O	11 - 2 M R X	6 + 4 N O T	9 - 3 B N S
10 - 0 S T O	5 + 5 P T H	3 + 3 C P T	3 + 7 E M B	4 - 1 D K V	1 + 9 E C A	8 + 2 U S E
12 - 2 T H E	5 - 1 G M Y	6 + 4 K I N	7 - 2 H N Z	1 x 10 G D O	6 + 1 B J M	3 + 7 M O F
5 x 2 H E A	8 - 2 C K N	4 + 6 V E N	2 + 8 B E L	7 + 1 F M Q	10 x 1 O N G	5 + 5 S T O
10 - 2 G N R	2 + 8 S U C	8 + 3 H P S	6 + 4 H A S	4 - 2 J Q T	7 + 3 T H E	11 - 1 S E

___ ___ _____ ____ __ __,

___ __ ___ ____ ____, _____

___ _____ __ _____ _____

__ ____ __ _____.

Complete the Story
Jesus Fed the People

Once Jesus went up on a mountain to preach to a great crowd of people. Near the end of the day the people were hungry. One of Jesus' disciples, Andrew, said there was a young boy in the crowd who had (a)_____ barley loaves and (b)_____ small fish. Jesus told his disciples to make all the people sit down in groups of (c)_____ and (d)_____. Then Jesus blessed the loaves and fish, and the disciples gave food to about (e)_____ people. After everyone had eaten, the disciples gathered (f)_____ baskets of food.

Work the arithmetic problems and then place your answers in the blanks above, matching the letters, to complete the story.

a. How many eyes you have.　　　　　　　　　_____
　　Add the number of days in a week.　　+　_____
　　Subtract number that rhymes with door.　−　_____
　　　　　　　　　　　　　Answer　_____

b. Number of months in a year.　　　　　_____
　　Subtract number that rhymes with pen.　−　_____
　　　　　　　　　　　　　Answer　_____

c. Number of minutes in an hour.　　　　_____
　　Subtract number of toes you have.　　−　_____
　　　　　　　　　　　　　Answer　_____

d. Number of feet you have.　　　　　　_____
　　Add number that sounds like ate.　　+　_____
　　Multiply by 10.　　　　　　　　　x　_____
　　　　　　　　　　　　　Answer　_____

e. Date of Christmas Day.　　　　　　　_____
　　Multiply by number of hands you have.　x　_____
　　Multiply by 100.　　　　　　　　x　_____
　　　　　　　　　　　　　Answer　_____

f. Write a number that rhymes with mix.　_____
　　Multiply by number of ears you have.　x　_____
　　　　　　　　　　　　　Answer　_____

Word Puzzle
Jesus Healed Two Blind Men

Two blind men who were sitting by the road heard that Jesus was passing by, so they began to shout, "Son of David! Have mercy on us!"

Jesus stopped and called out, "What do you want me to do for you?"

Sir," they said, "we want you to give us our sight!"

Jesus had pity on them and touched their eyes; at once they were able to see, and they followed him.

Place the underlined words in the puzzle blanks. The word list will help you.

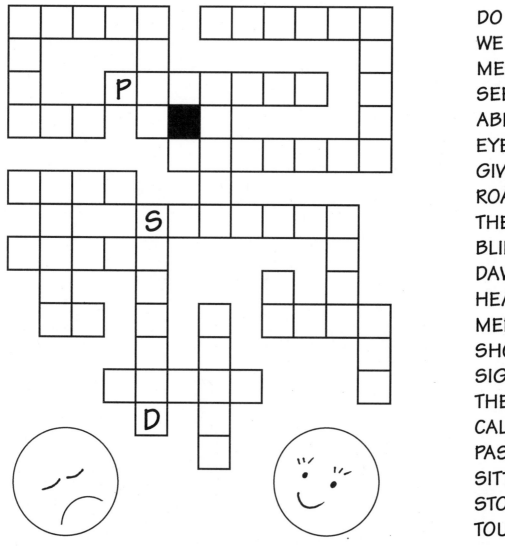

DO
WE
MEN
SEE
ABLE
EYES
GIVE
ROAD
THEM
BLIND
DAVID
HEARD
MERCY
SHOUT
SIGHT
THEIR
CALLED
PASSING
SITTING
STOPPED
TOUCHED

A Sycamore Tree
Jesus Was a Friend to Zacchaeus

A man named Zacchaeus wanted to see Jesus, but he was very short and could not see over the heads of the crowd. So Zacchaeus climbed up into a sycamore tree. When Jesus came to the tree, he looked up and saw Zacchaeus. The puzzle will tell you what Jesus said.

Write a word for each definition. Then write the letters in the puzzle blanks on the tree matching the numbers.

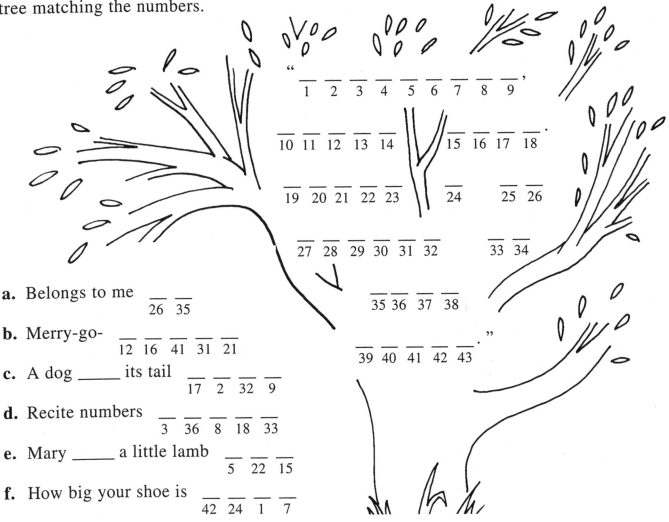

"— — — — — — — — — ,
 1 2 3 4 5 6 7 8 9

— — — — — — — — — .
10 11 12 13 14   15 16 17 18

— — — — — — — —
19 20 21 22 23 24   25 26

— — — — — — — —
27 28 29 30 31 32   33 34

— — — —
35 36 37 38

— — — — — ."
39 40 41 42 43

a. Belongs to me — —
                      26 35

b. Merry-go- — — — — —
                 12 16 41 31 21

c. A dog ____ its tail — — — —
                          17 2 32 9

d. Recite numbers — — — — —
                      3 36 8 18 33

e. Mary ____ a little lamb — — —
                              5 22 15

f. How big your shoe is — — — —
                           42 24 1 7

g. Animal with ringed tail — — — — — — —
                              13 25 4 27 34 40 18

h. It covers your head — — — —
                          10 6 30 38

i. Opposite of me — — —
                      14 28 37

j. You put food in your — — — — —
                           29 20 11 19 39

k. The way people used to say "you" — —
                                        23 43

35

A Story in Braille
Jesus and Bartimaeus

At the time Jesus was on earth, blind people were often ragged and hungry and had to beg for food. One blind man's name was Bartimaeus. He heard that Jesus was coming. The Braille code, used by blind people today, will tell you what happened.

A B C D E F G H I J K L M N O P Q R S T U

V W X Y Z

Bartimaeus:

Jesus:

Bartimaeus:

Jesus:

36

Place the Letters

Choose to Follow Jesus

When Jesus was on earth, many people chose to follow him. Below are the names of some of those people. Use the list to write the names in the correct places. (The first one is done for you.) Then place the circled letters in the sentence to read something just for you.

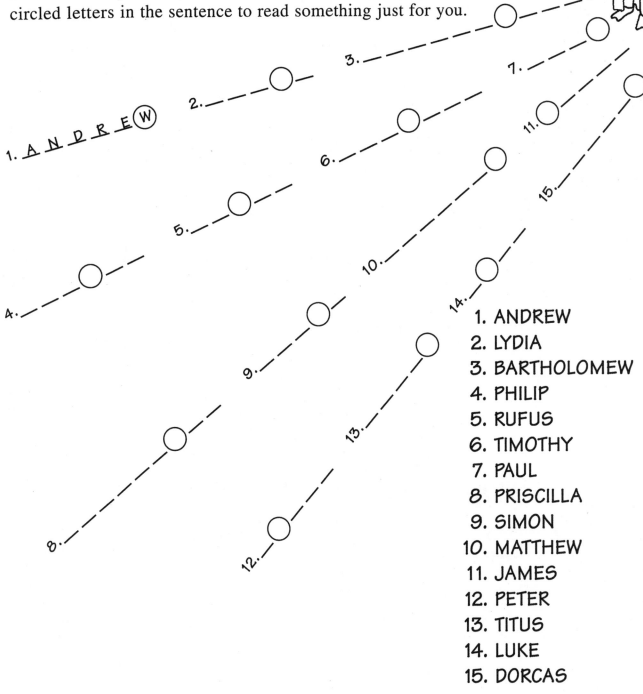

1. A N D R E (W)

1. ANDREW
2. LYDIA
3. BARTHOLOMEW
4. PHILIP
5. RUFUS
6. TIMOTHY
7. PAUL
8. PRISCILLA
9. SIMON
10. MATTHEW
11. JAMES
12. PETER
13. TITUS
14. LUKE
15. DORCAS

_____   W __ __ __   __ __ __ __ __ __   __ __ __ __ __ .
Write your name here.   1 2 3 4   5 6 7 8 9 10   11 12 13 14 15

Words in the Temple
Choose to Speak Up

Even when Jesus was a boy, he spoke up about his heavenly Father. Once, after the Feast of the Passover at Jerusalem, Joseph and Mary found Jesus in the temple, listening to the priests and asking them questions. Joseph and Mary asked Jesus why he was there. To find his answer, fit the list of words into the squares in the temple. Then arrange them by number in the sentence.

a. look
b. house
c. Father's
d. Why
e. know
f. that
g. Didn't

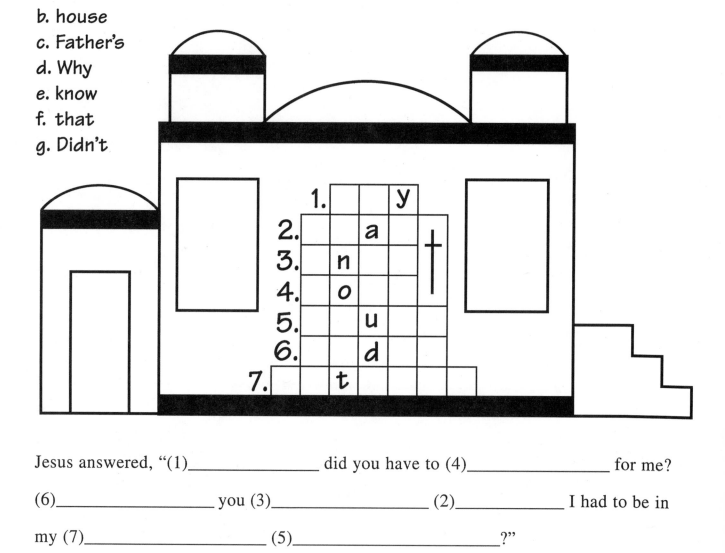

Jesus answered, "(1)_____ did you have to (4)_____ for me?

(6)_____ you (3)_____ (2)_____ I had to be in

my (7)_____ (5)_____?"

List some ways you can speak up for Jesus.

38

A Picture Puzzle

Choose to Help Others

When we help others (are merciful to them), it means that we are being used to do God's work. In Matthew 5:3-11, we can read some verses called the Beatitudes. The puzzle below will tell you what Jesus said in one Beatitude.

Follow the directions, adding and subtracting the letters of the objects shown. Place the words in the blanks to complete the sentence.

BLUE + STARS − RAT + RED − U R =

1._____

SHOE + DOOR − FOOT + BALL + L − LAMB =

2._____

" __ __ __ __ __ __ __ are the merciful: for they __ __ __ __ __ obtain mercy."
                    1   2

Write some ways you can help others.

A Special Clock
A Time for Everything

The book of Ecclesiastes tells us there is a time for everything.

Match the scrambled words on the clock to the correct words in the list, and place the correct number beside each word. Draw clock hands to two things you think are most important.

HARVEST ____   SPEAK ____   LOVE ____   BUILD UP ____
LAUGH ____   PEACE ____   DANCE ____   KEEP ____
BORN ____   HEAL ____   PLANT ____   CRY ____

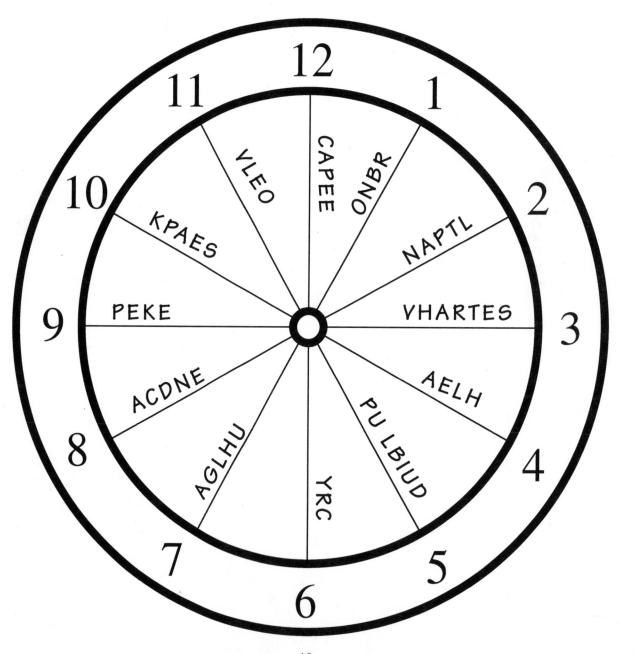

Coded Words
"The Gospel in a Nutshell"

One night a man named Nicodemus asked Jesus about God's love. Use the code to solve the puzzle and discover what Jesus told Nicodemus. The answer is called "The Gospel in a Nutshell," and all who believe it belong to God's family.

Code: A B C D E F G H I J K L M N O P Q R S T U V W X Y Z
   1 2 3 4 5 6 7 8 9 10 11 12 13 14 15 16 17 18 19 20 21 22 23 24 25 26

___ ___,
6 15 18 7 15 4 19 15 12 15 22 5 4 20 8 5 23 15 18 12 4

___ ___ ___ ___ ___ ___ ___ ___ ___ ___ ___ ___ ___ ___ ___ ___ ___
20 8 1 20 8 5 7 1 22 5 8 9 19 15 14 12 25

___ ___ ___ ___ ___ ___ ___ ___ ___ ___ ___ ___, ___ ___ ___ ___ ___ ___ ___ ___ ___ ___ ___ ___ ___ ___
2 5 7 15 20 20 5 14 19 15 14 20 8 1 20 23 8 15 19 15 5 22 5 18

___ ___ ___ ___ ___ ___ ___ ___ ___ ___ ___ ___ ___ ___ ___ ___ ___ ___ ___ ___
2 5 12 9 5 22 5 20 8 9 14 8 9 13 19 8 15 21 12 4

___ ___ ___ ___ ___ ___ ___ ___ ___, ___ ___ ___ ___ ___ ___ ___
14 15 20 16 5 18 9 19 8 2 21 20 8 1 22 5

___ ___ ___ ___ ___ ___ ___ ___ ___ ___ ___ ___ ___ ___ ___. John 3:16 (KJV)
5 22 5 18 12 1 19 20 9 14 7 12 9 6 5

Match the Numbers
Living as Believers

The apostle Paul wrote letters to churches. He encouraged the members to live as believers in Christ. There are many Bible verses that tell us how to live as believers. Work the puzzle to read one of those verses.

Write a word for each definition. Then transfer the letters to the blanks in the Bible verse, matching the numbers. (The first one is done for you.)

a. The Bible verse below is found in $\underset{24}{C}\ \underset{37}{O}\ \underset{76}{R}\ \underset{40}{I}\ \underset{74}{N}\ \underset{13}{T}\ \underset{61}{H}\ \underset{4}{I}\ \underset{80}{A}\ \underset{51}{N}\ \underset{30}{S}$.

b. A believer has $\overline{7}\ \overline{82}\ \overline{27}\ \overline{45}\ \overline{70}$.

c. He was in the lion's den $\overline{6}\ \overline{73}\ \overline{36}\ \overline{23}\ \overline{19}\ \overline{39}$.

d. From beginning to end $\overline{16}\ \overline{31}\ \overline{68}\ \overline{77}\ \overline{50}\ \overline{81}\ \overline{58}$

e. Period of time, or in a $\overline{21}\ \overline{14}\ \overline{83}\ \overline{11}\ \overline{64}$

f. A glass container $\overline{47}\ \overline{67}\ \overline{17}\ \overline{38}\ \overline{26}\ \overline{42}$

g. Another name for father $\overline{35}\ \overline{10}\ \overline{62}\ \overline{75}\ \overline{20}$

h. A large cat $\overline{60}\ \overline{54}\ \overline{29}\ \overline{71}\ \overline{52}\ \overline{15}\ \overline{25}$

i. Part of the face $\overline{56}\ \overline{8}\ \overline{33}\ \overline{49}\ \overline{18}$

j. To lower the noise, you turn down the $\overline{28}\ \overline{32}\ \overline{12}\ \overline{43}\ \overline{72}\ \overline{2}$.

k. Another word for "supper" $\overline{65}\ \overline{55}\ \overline{44}\ \overline{84}\ \overline{5}\ \overline{9}$

l. I _____ if I could! $\overline{57}\ \overline{53}\ \overline{48}\ \overline{11}\ \overline{3}$

m. Jesus fed five thousand people with two $\overline{66}\ \overline{59}\ \overline{78}\ \overline{22}$ and some bread.

n. Small lavender flower $\overline{41}\ \overline{63}\ \overline{46}\ \overline{34}\ \overline{79}\ \overline{69}$

$\underset{1}{H}\ \overline{2}\quad \overline{3}\ \underset{4}{I}\ \overline{5}\ \overline{6}\quad \overline{7}\ \overline{8}\ \overline{9},\quad \overline{10}\ \overline{11}\ \overline{12}\quad \underset{13}{T}\ \overline{14}\ \overline{15}\ \overline{16}\quad \overline{17}\ \overline{18}\ \overline{19}\ \overline{20}$

$\overline{21}\ \overline{22}\ \overline{23}\ \underset{24}{C}\ \overline{25}\quad \overline{26}\ \overline{27}\ \overline{28}\ \overline{29}\quad \underset{30}{S}\ \overline{31}\ \overline{32}\ \overline{33}\ \overline{34}\ \overline{35}\quad \overline{36}\ \underset{37}{O}\ \overline{38}$

$\underset{39}{H}\ \underset{}{E}\ \underset{}{N}\ \underset{}{C}\ \underset{}{E}\ \underset{}{F}\ \underset{}{O}\ \underset{}{R}\ \underset{}{T}\ \underset{}{H}\quad \underset{39}{}\ \underset{40}{I}\ \overline{41}\ \overline{42}\quad \overline{43}\ \overline{44}\ \overline{45}\ \overline{46}$

HENCEFORTH $\overline{39}\ \underset{40}{I}\ \overline{41}\ \overline{42}\quad \overline{43}\ \overline{44}\ \overline{45}\ \overline{46}$

THEMSELVES, $\overline{47}\ \overline{48}\ \overline{49}\quad \overline{50}\ \underset{51}{N}\ \overline{52}\ \overline{53}\quad \overline{54}\ \overline{55}\ \overline{56}$

$\overline{57}\ \overline{58}\ \overline{59}\ \overline{60}\ \underset{61}{H}\quad \overline{62}\ \overline{63}\ \overline{64}\ \overline{65}\quad \overline{66}\ \overline{67}\ \overline{68}\quad \overline{69}\ \overline{70}\ \overline{71}\ \overline{72},\quad \overline{73}\ \underset{74}{N}\ \overline{75}$

$\underset{76}{R}\ \overline{77}\ \overline{78}\ \overline{79}\quad \underset{80}{A}\ \overline{81}\ \overline{82}\ \overline{83}\ \overline{84}$.

Word Search
The Great Mission Command

The disciples went to a mountain in Galilee where Jesus asked them to come together. He told them the gospel is for all the world. His words, called "The Great Mission Command," are written in Matthew 28:18-20 (KJV). Read the verses, write the words in the blanks, then find those words in the puzzle maze. Words can be horizontal, vertical, diagonal, backward, or forward.

And Jesus came and _____ unto _____, _____, All

_____ is _____ unto me in _____ and in _____.

Go ye _____, and _____ all _____, _____

them in the _____ of the _____, and of the _____, and of the _____

_____: _____ them to _____ all things _____ I

_____ _____ you: and, lo, I am with you _____,

even _____ the end of the _____.

```
        A U G
      T N E M S B
      T E M B H N D
    O S P A K E L T
  C I O P N C R U Y G
  D J T T S O H G N L P
V E I K Q W M W I F L O
R Z X T H E M Y G N M S H
Y I S N O I T A N H P G N C
N O E T Z I S N O S O N U A
G I V E N C L R D Y A W L A E X
D H A V E M O B S E R V E A R T H
R E H T A F A J P D V B R K Q W B
W H A T S O E V E R O F E R E H T X
```

A Message in Morse Code
"Love One Another"

The Bible says, in 1 John 4:8, that "God is love." Below are some messages about love, but they are in Morse code. Use the code key to "unlock" the answers.

A B C D E F G H I J K L M N O P Q

R S T U V W X Y Z

1. Whom should we love?

2. How should we love?

3. Why should we love?

4. How much should we love?

5. Is anything more important than love?

44

Use the Code
How Much God Loves Us

How much does God love us? What did God do for us? What does God want us to do? Use the code to read the words that will answer the questions. Find the matching part of the grid; one dot means the answer is the first letter, two dots mean it's the second, etc. For example, ___•⌋ = a, ___••⌋ = b, •••⌋ = c. Write your answer on the lines above the code symbols. Perhaps you would like to use the code to write a message of your own.

A	B	C	D	E	F	G	H	I
J	K	L	M	N	O	P	Q	R
S	T	U	V	W	X	Y	Z	

Find the Words
The Twenty-third Psalm

The Twenty-third Psalm is called the Shepherd Psalm. Look it up in the Bible (King James Version) and write the missing words in the blanks. Then find those words in the puzzle square. Words in puzzle square may be across, down or diagonal, backward or forward. (An example is circled.) You might like to memorize this psalm.

The Lord is my _____; I shall not want. He maketh me to lie down in

_____ _____: he _____ me

_____ the still waters. He restoreth my _____: he leadeth me in the

_____ of righteousness for his name's sake. Yea, though I walk through the

_____ of the _____ of death, I will fear no evil: for thou art with me;

thy rod and thy _____ they _____ me. Thou preparest a _____

_____ me in the presence of _____ enemies: thou anointest my head

with oil; my cup _____ over. Surely goodness and _____ shall

_____ me all the _____ of my life: and I will _____ in the

_____ of the _____ for ever.

```
W  O  L  L  O  F  B  M  I  N  E  G
Y  S  T  R  O  F  M  O  C  L  M  S
C  O  R  W  L  A  C  H  B  N  S  H
R  U  N  N  E  T  H  A  V  D  Y  E
E  L  J  P  A  S  T  U  R  E  S  P
M  E  P  T  D  W  S  N  L  F  A  H
K  D  Q  A  E  V  H  L  E  T  X  E
B  I  Y  L  T  L  A  R  H  E  W  R
E  S  U  O  H  V  D  S  Y  C  R  D
G  E  L  R  E  R  O  F  E  B  P  G
A  B  H  D  M  D  W  E  L  L  C  Q
```

46

Follow the Arrows

"All Authority"

Once Jesus told his disciples, "I have been given all authority in heaven and on earth" (Matthew 28:18). Many other Bible verses tell us that Jesus Christ is the head of the church. Follow the arrows and write the words on the lines beneath each puzzle.

Start

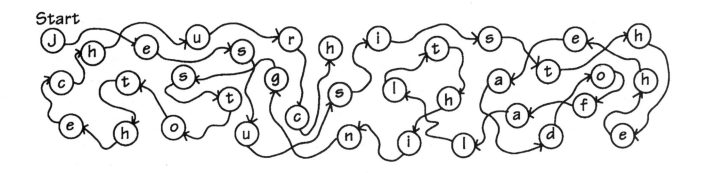

_____

_____

Start

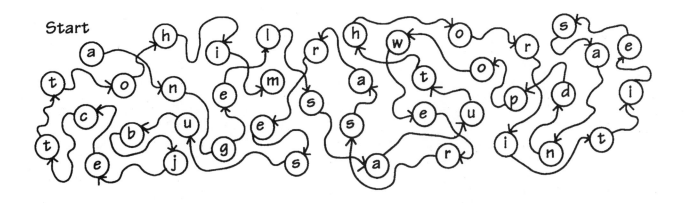

_____

_____

Which Day?
We Are God's Creation

In the first chapter of the first book of the Bible, Genesis, you can read the story of how God created the world. Number the pictures below according to the day on which God created each of the things pictured.

a. ___ trees

b. ___ people

c. ___ light, darkness

d. ___ birds

e. ___ moon, stars

f. ___ animals

g. ___ earth

h. ___ sky

i. ___ fish

j.___ flowers

k. ___ cattle

l. ___ sun

Find It–Fill It In

We Are Caretakers for God

A caretaker is a person who takes care of something. God has given us many things and wants us to take care of them. Follow the directions below to find out more about caretakers.

The 5th letter of the alphabet _____
It's in BEAT but not in BET _____
Letter after Q _____
A letter that sounds like a drink _____
Letter before I _____

1. List the things you can do to help take care of the _____.

Use the word you found here to complete sentence 1.

The 16th letter of alphabet _____
It's in LEAD but not in LAD _____
Letter that looks like a circle _____
Letter before Q _____
It's in SLIP but not in SIP _____
The 5th letter of alphabet _____

2. List things you can do to help take care of _____.

Use the word you found here to complete sentence 2.

Next to last letter of alphabet _____
Letter after N _____
Letter that sounds opposite of ME _____
Letter before S _____
It's in THIS but not in HIT _____
Letter before F _____
The 12th letter of alphabet _____
It's in FATE, but not in EAT _____

3. List things you can do to take care of _____.

Use the word you found here to complete sentence 3.

Cross out the extra letters in the following Bible verse that tells why we should be caretakers for God.

C L O R D , D N R T H E T C E A R T H B L Z O M F J I S N G F U L L W H K O F
X N Y O U R B N T C O N S T A N T C Y J L O V E.   Psalm 119:64

An Old Custom
We Take Care of Others

It was the custom for Israelite farmers to leave some stalks of grain in the field for poor people. Picking up the leftover grain was called gleaning. How did this custom begin? Work the puzzle to finish reading what God said.

Fill in the blanks to complete the thoughts. Then transfer the letters to the blanks in the Bible verse, using matching numbers.

a. To give food to is to ___ ___ ___ ___.
26 18 22 25

b. You swim in a ___ ___ ___ ___.
13 27 11 21

c. Person you play with ___ ___ ___ ___ ___ ___
10 16 30 5 24 25

d. It twinkles at night ___ ___ ___ ___
35 6 3 28

e. Jesus went up to ___ ___ ___ ___ ___ ___.
7 33 23 4 29 32

f. Bride and ___ ___ ___ ___ ___
31 12 27 15 9

g. The rug is on the ___ ___ ___ ___ ___.
26 1 14 19 34

h. Salt and ___ ___ ___ ___ ___ ___
17 8 20 13 2 28

God said, "When you harvest your fields, do not cut the grain at the edges of the fields, and do not go back to cut the heads of grain that were left;

___ ___ ___ ___ ___   ___ ___ ___ ___   ___ ___ ___
1 2 3 4 5   6 7 8 9   10 11 12

___ ___ ___ ___   ___ ___ ___ ___ ___ ___   ___ ___ ___
13 14 15 16   17 18 19 20 21 22   23 24 25

___ ___ ___ ___ ___ ___ ___ ___ ___ ___ ."
26 27 28 29 30 31 32 33 34 35

Words at the Well
We Are All Brothers and Sisters

The Israelites and Samaritans were not very friendly to each other, but Jesus treated everyone as a sister or brother. Once he was traveling through the country of Samaria, and he stopped at a well for a drink of water. Read John 4:6-28 to see what happened. Then number the events in the stones in the order in which they happened.

1. ____
2. ____
3. ____
4. ____
5. ____
6. ____
7. ____
8. ____
9. ____
10. ____

A. Jesus said "I am he."

B. Jesus said, "God is Spirit."

C. The woman said, "I have no husband."

D. A woman of Samaria came to the well.

E. Jesus rested at Jacob's well.

G. The woman said "I know that the Messiah will come."

F. The woman said "I see you are a prophet."

H. Jesus said, "You do not know whom you worship."

I. The woman said, "Could he be the Messiah?"

J. Jesus said, "Whoever drinks the water I give will never be thirsty again."

How many words can you make with the letters in the word SAMARITAN?

_____ _____ _____ _____

_____ _____ _____ _____

_____ _____ _____ _____

_____ _____ _____ _____

_____ _____ _____ _____

Build a Church
Our Church Family

The Bible tells us to love others. But sometimes we are not loving, and cause others trouble. Unscramble the letters to find the problems that divide the church. Write the words on the lines next to church number 1. Do the same for church number 2 to list the blessings that keep the church whole. Look up 2 Corinthians 12:20 and Galatians 5:22 if you need help.

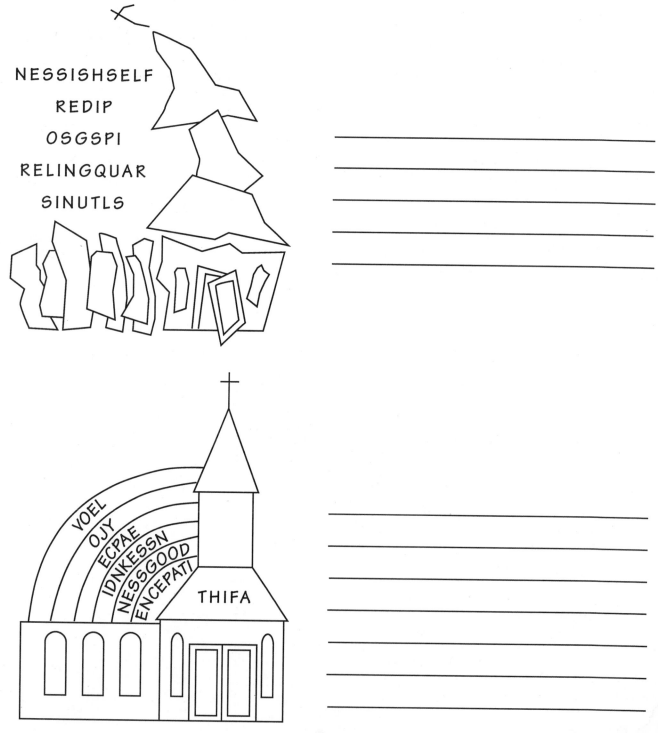

NESSISHSELF

REDIP

OSGSPI

RELINGQUAR

SINUTLS

_____

_____

_____

_____

_____

VOEL

OJY

ECPAE

IDNKESSN

NESSGOOD

ENCEPATI

THIFA

_____

_____

_____

_____

_____

_____

Word Pyramids
Our World Family

When we think of family, we usually think of our parents, sisters and brothers, aunts and uncles. But Jesus said we have a much larger family.

Read Matthew 12:46-50 and then fill in the words in the pyramids, using the verse numbers as a guide.

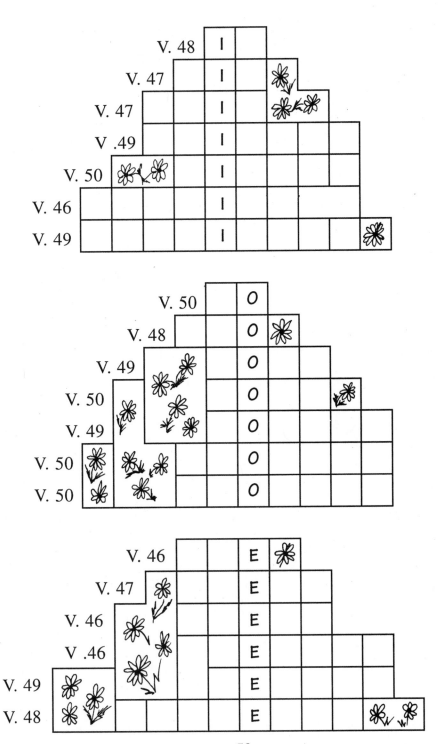

Decode It!
The Lord's Prayer

Once Jesus gave a talk called "The Sermon on the Mount." Part of that sermon was the Lord's Prayer. Use the code to write the prayer. You might like to memorize it.

Code: A = B, B= C, C = D, etc.

NTQ   E   SGDQ   VGHBG   QS   HM   GD   UDM,   G   KKNVDC
___   _   ____   _____   __   __   __   ___   _   _____
      A   A   A   ,   A

AD   SGX   M   LD.   SGX   JHMFCNL   BNLD.   SGX   VHKK   AD
__   ___   _   __.   ___   _____   ____.   ___   ____   __
           A

CNMD   HM   D   QSG,   R   HS   HR   HM   GD   UDM.   FHUD   TR
____   __   _   ___,   _   __   __   __   __   ___.   ____   __
            A   ,   A   A

SGHR   C   X   NTQ   C   HKX   AQD   C.   MC   ENQFHUD   TR
____   _   _   ___   _   ___   ___   _.   __   _____   __
       A   A   A . A

NTQ   CDASR,   R   VD   ENQFHUD   NTQ   CDASNQR.   MC
___   _____,   _   __   _____   ___   _____.   __
          ,   A   . A

KD   C   TR   MNS   HMSN   SDLOS   SHNM,   ATS   CDKHUDQ
__   _   __   ___   ____   _____   ____,   ___   _____
     A   A   ,

TR   EQNL   DUHK: ENQ   SGHMD   HR   SGD   JHMFCNL,
__   ____   ____: ___   _____   __   ___   _____,
            :   ,

MC   SGD   ONVDQ,   MC   SGD   FKNQX,   ENQ   DUDQ.
__   ___   _____,   __   ___   _____,   ___   ____.
A   ,   A   ,

                                             L DM.
                                             ____.
                                             A

Use the code to write a prayer of your own.

54

Put the Words in Order
Baptism and Communion

Write, in numerical order, all of the words in the baptism shells to read something Jesus said about baptism.

"1. _____ 2. and 3. _____ 4. _____

　　　5. _____ 6. and 7. _____

8. _____ 9. _____ 10. _____."

8. will　　4. and　　6. bapt　　2. belie

3. ves　　5. is　　7. ized　　10. saved　　1. Whoever　　9. be

The night before Jesus was arrested, he did something special with his disciples. Find number 1 in the Communion cup, then number 2, and so on. Write the numbered words in the spaces at the end of the sentence to read what happened.

Jesus took bread, blessed it, broke it and gave it to the disciples. He said,

"1._____ 2._____ …3._____ 4._____ _____ 5._____."

He took the cup, and gave thanks, and gave it to them, and they all drank of it. He said,

"6._____7.____ _____ 8._____ 9._____ 10._____

　11._____ 12._____ 13. _____ 14. _____."

8. blood　　3. this　　14. many　　11. poured　　5. body　　9. which　　2. it

4. is my　　12. out　　6. This　　10. is　　1. Take　　13. for　　7. is my

55

Read the Music

Singing Praises

The psalms in the Bible were once used as hymns. Some hymns we sing today are based on the psalms. The puzzle below is Psalm 100 (King James Version). Fill in the missing letters by reading the notes as follows:

[Musical staff with treble clef showing notes labeled F G A B C D E]

M[a]K[e] a joyful noise unto the LOR[d] [a]LL Y[e] L[a]N[d]S.

S[e]RV[e] the LOR[d] with [g]L[ad]N[e]SS. [c]OM[e] [bef]OR[e] his

PR[e]S[e]N[ce] with singing. Know Y[e] that the Lord he is [g]O[d]: it is

H[e] that hath M[ade] us [a]N[d] not W[e] ourselves; W[e] [a]R[e]

his people [a]N[d] the SH[ee]P of his pasture. [e]NT[e]R into his

[ga]T[e]S with thanksgiving [a]N[d] into his courts with praise:

[be] thankful unto him [a]N[d] [b]L[e]SS his N[a]M[e].

For the LOR[d] is [g]OO[d]: his M[e]R[c]Y is everlasting;

[a]N[d] his truth endureth to [a]LL [ge]N[e]R[a]TIONS.

56

Answers

Fill In the Blanks
p. 7

Old Testament books.
- a. 4
- b. 7
- c. 5
- d. 9
- e. 2
- f. 6
- g. 8
- h. 1
- i. 10
- j. 3

New Testament books
1. Hebrews
2. Acts
3. Luke
4. Mark
5. John
6. Revelation
7. Matthew
8. Jude

Putting Things in Order
p. 8

Aaron—person
Adam—person
Ararat—place
Covenant—thing
Edom—place
Galilee—place
Goshen—place
Hannah—person
Jasper—thing
Marble—thing
Moriah—place
Moses—person
Onyx—thing
Patmos—place
Scapegoat—thing
Shiloh—place
Talmud—thing
Topaz—thing
Willow—thing
Zechariah—person

Look It Up!
p. 9

1. Book of Jonah
2. Matthew 6:9-13
3. 1 John 4:8
4. Psalm 23:2
5. Isaiah 40:31
6. Matthew 28:19
7. Hebrews 11:33
8. John 20:16

Connect the Words
p. 10

1. garden
2. not
3. tree
4. evil
5. Lord
6. die
7. eyes
8. serpent
9. thereof
10. fig leaves
11. shouldest
12. thee
13. enmity
14. ye
15. eat
16. thistles
17. sorrow
18. wise

Figure It Out!
p. 11

1. 600
2. 450
3. 75
4. 45
5. 3
6. 2
7. 40
8. 7
9. 10
10. 14 (Genesis 6–8)
rainbow (Genesis 9:13)

Fit the Words
p. 12

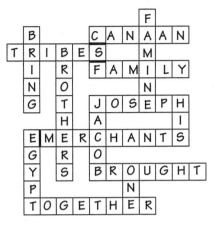

See Genesis 42–43.

Climb the Mountain
p. 13

MOUNT
1. mound
2. sound
3. downs
4. winds
5. rinds
6. rains
7. Sinai

See Exodus 19:20.

WATER
1. tears
2. steak
3. stack
4. stick

See Numbers 20:11.

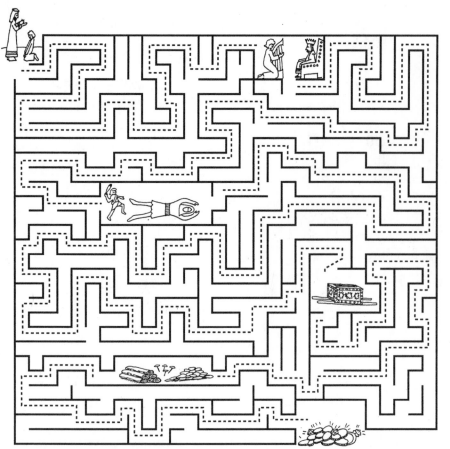

Find the Way
p. 15

1. Samuel blessed David.
2. David played the harp for King Saul.
3. David killed the giant, Goliath.
4. David took the Ark (Covenant Box) of the Lord to Jerusalem.
5. David gathered cedarwood, iron for nails, and stones fitted for God's temple.
6. David collected gold, silver, brass, and iron for the temple and treasury.

A Prayer in Code
p. 14

"The Lord has filled my heart with joy; how happy I am because of what he has done! I laugh at my enemies; how joyful I am because God has helped me! No one is holy like the Lord; there is none like him."

1 Samuel 2:1-2a

Make A Map
p. 16

1. Simeon
2. Judah
3. Dan
4. Benjamin
5. Ephraim
6. Manasseh
7. Issachar
8. Zebulun
9. Asher
10. Naphtali
11. Gad
12. Reuben

Use the Clues
p. 17

a. Shadrach
b. Meshach
c. Abednego

See Daniel 3:19-26.

Write the Words
p. 18

1. men
2. peach
3. king
4. beet
5. Peter
6. left
7. duck
8. red
9. jelly
10. up
11. apple
12. ship
13. cat
14. Lord's
15. last
16. tin
17. candy

Words in squares:
mene tekel upharsin

See Daniel 5:25-26 (KJV).

A Ladder to Climb
p. 19

1. Canaan
2. night
3. traveling
4. Bethel
5. Lord
6. descending
7. slept
8. angel
9. named
10. place
11. Haran

See Genesis 28:5-19.

A Promise in the Stars
p. 20

"I promise that I will give you as many descendants as there are stars in the sky or grains of sand along the seashore."

Genesis 22:17

It's a Maze
p. 22

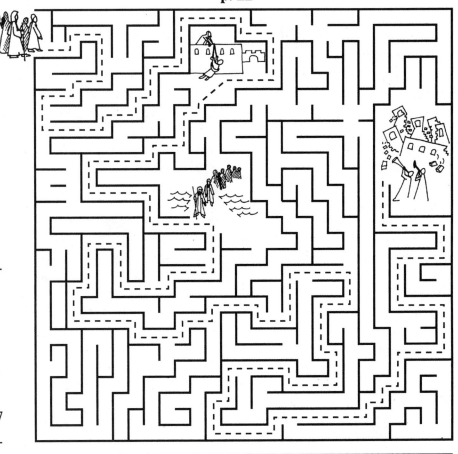

Fill In the Words
p. 21

a. baked
b. fell down
c. sailing
d. moonlight
e. underneath
f. fawn
g. hill
h. town
i. eagle
j. tiny
k. me

God said, "I will send an angel before thee...unto a land flowing with milk and honey."

Exodus 33:2-3 (KJV)

Unscramble the Scrambles
p. 23

v.46 magnify
v.47 spirit, Saviour
v.48 estate, behold, blessed
v.49 mighty, great
v.50 mercy, fear
v.51 strength, proud, hearts
v.52 down, seats
v.53 hungry, empty
v.54 Israel, mercy
v.55 fathers, seed

Letters to Add and Subtract
p. 24

1. country
2. Bethlehem
3. studied
4. stars
5. King
6. Herod
7. east
8. worship
9. gold
10. frankincense
11. myrrh

See Matthew 2:1-5.

Circle Words
p. 25
You did not choose me; I chose you, and appointed you to go and bear much fruit, the kind of fruit that endures. And so the Father will give you whatever you ask of him in my name.

See John 15:16.

Disciples' names:
1. James
2. Peter
3. Matthew
4. Thomas
5. Simon
6. Philip
7. John
8. James
9. Thaddaeus
10. Andrew

Boxed name: Bartholomew

Missing disciple: Judas

1,2,3...
p. 26
When Jesus was teaching and preaching, Joanna and many other women supported his work and helped him. On Easter morning, Joanna and some other women went to the tomb where Jesus had been placed after he was crucified. The tomb was empty, and an angel told them Jesus was alive.

See Luke 24:1-7.

Picture Clues
p. 27
An angel of the Lord told Philip to go to the road that went from Jerusalem to Gaza. Philip found a man who was reading the book of Isaiah. The Holy Spirit told Philip to explain God's Word to the man. Philip told the man about Jesus. Then the man said, "There is some water. Please baptize me." After he was baptized the Holy Spirit took Philip away. The man went to his house rejoicing. (Picture words are underlined.)

See Acts 8:26-39.

Combine the Letters
p. 28
Peter was kept in prison. The angel of the Lord came and Peter's chains fell off his hands. They came to the iron gate which opened. They passed to one street and the angel left. Peter explained how the Lord had brought him out of prison.

See Acts 12:6-17.

Rhyme Puzzles
p. 29
1. Thyatira
2. preach
3. baptized
4. house

See Acts 16:14-15.

A House of Words
p. 30
1. son
2. who
3. sins
4. pick
5. only
6. home
7. healed
8. forgive

See Mark 2:4-12.

Big and Little Letters
p. 31
Samaria
leprosy
voices
Master
priests
healed

See Luke 17:11-19.

Find the Tens
p. 32
Let the children come to me, and do not stop them, because the Kingdom of heaven belongs to such as these.
                    Matthew 19:14

Complete the Story
p. 33
a. 2 + 7 - 4 = 5
b. 12 - 10 = 2
c. 60 - 10 = 50
d. 2 + 8 x 10 = 100
e. 25 x 2 x 100 = 5000
f. 6 x 2 = 12

See John 6:3-14.

Word Puzzle
p. 34

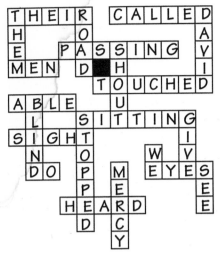

See Matthew 20:30-34.

A Sycamore Tree
p. 35

a. my
b. round
c. wags
d. count
e. had
f. size
g. raccoon
h. hair
i. you
j. mouth
k. ye

"Zacchaeus, hurry down. Today I am coming to your house."

See Luke 19: 1-10.

A Story in Braille
p. 36

Bartimaeus: Jesus! Son of David! Have mercy on me!

Jesus: What do you want me to do for you?

Bartimaeus: Teacher, I want to see.

Jesus: Go, your faith has made you well.

See Mark 10.

Place the Letters
p. 37

Letters in the circles spell the message, (child's name) will follow Jesus.

_____

Words in the Temple
p. 38

1. Why
2. that
3. know
4. look
5. house
6. Didn't
7. Father's

"Why did you have to look for me? Didn't you know that I had to be in my Father's house?"

Luke 2:40-52

_____

A Picture Puzzle
p. 39

1. blue + stars - rat + red - UR = blessed
2. shoe + mat - toe + ball + L - lamb = shall

Matthew 5:7 (KJV)

_____

A Special Clock
p. 40

1. born
2. plant
3. harvest
4. heal
5. build up
6. cry
7. laugh
8. dance
9. keep
10. speak
11. love
12. peace

See Ecclesiastes 3:1-8.

Coded Words
p. 41

For God so loved the world, that he gave his only begotten Son, that whosoever believeth in him should not perish, but have everlasting life.

John 3:16 (KJV)

_____

Match the Numbers
p. 42

a. Corinthians
b. faith
c. Daniel
d. through
e. while
f. bottle
g. daddy
h. cheetah
i. mouth
j. volume
k. dinner
l. would
m. fish
n. violet

Bible verse: He died for all, that they which live should not henceforth live unto themselves, but unto him which died for them, and rose again.

2 Corinthians 5:15 (KJV)

Word Search
p. 43

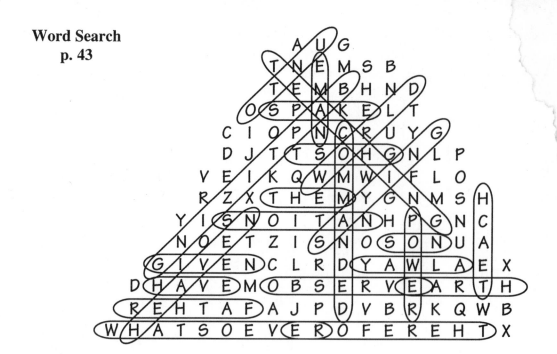

A Message in Morse Code
p. 44

1. One another and all people.
   1 Thessalonians 3:12

2. Love your neighbor as yourself.
   Matthew 22:39

3. Because God first loved us.
   1 John 4:19

4. Love the Lord with all your heart and soul and strength.
   Deuteronomy 6:5

5. Faith, hope, and love: the greatest of these is love.
   1 Corinthians 13:13

Use the Code
p. 45

Herein is love, not that we loved God, but that he loved us, and sent his Son to be the propitiation for our sins. Beloved, if God so loved us, we ought also to love one another.
   1 John 4:10-11 (KJV)

Find the Words
p. 46

shepherd
green pastures
leadeth
beside
soul
paths
valley
shadow
staff
comfort
table
before
mine
runneth
mercy
follow
days
dwell
house
Lord

Follow the Arrows
p. 47

Jesus is the head of all things to the church.

See Ephesians 1:22.

Angels, authorities, and powers are subject to him.

See 1 Peter 3:22.

Which Day?
p. 48

a. 3
b. 6
c. 1
d. 5
e. 4
f. 6
g. 3
h. 2
i. 5
j. 3
k. 6
l. 4

Find It—Fill It In
p. 49

1. earth
2. people
3. yourself

LORD, ~~DNR~~ THE ~~TC~~ EARTH ~~BLZOCMFJ~~ IS ~~NG~~ FULL ~~WIK~~ OF ~~XN~~ YOUR ~~BNT~~ CONSTANT ~~CYJ~~ LOVE.

Psalm 119:64

An Old Custom
p. 50

a. feed
b. pool
c. friend
d. star
e. heaven
f. groom
g. floor
h. pepper

Bible verse
"…leave them for poor people and foreigners."

Leviticus 23:22

Words at the Well
p. 51

1. e
2. d
3. j
4. c
5. f
6. h
7. b
8. g
9. a
10. i

Build a Church
p. 52

1. pride
   gossip
   selfishness
   quarreling
   insults

2. love
   joy
   peace
   kindness
   goodness
   patience
   faith

Word Pyramids
p. 53

is
him
said
pointed
sister
outside
disciples

do
who
look
does
mother
brother
whoever

the
there
speak
people
heaven
answered

Decode It!
p. 54

Matthew 6:9-13 (KJV)

Put the Words in Order
p. 55

"Take it…this is my body."
"This is my blood which is poured out for many."

Mark 14:22-24

"Whoever believes and is baptized will be saved."

Mark 16:16

Read the Music
p. 56

Make
Lord
all
ye
lands
Serve
Lord
gladness
Come
before
presence
ye
God
he
made
and
we
we
are
and
sheep
Enter
gates
and
be
and
bless
name
Lord
good
mercy
and
all
generations

Read the Music